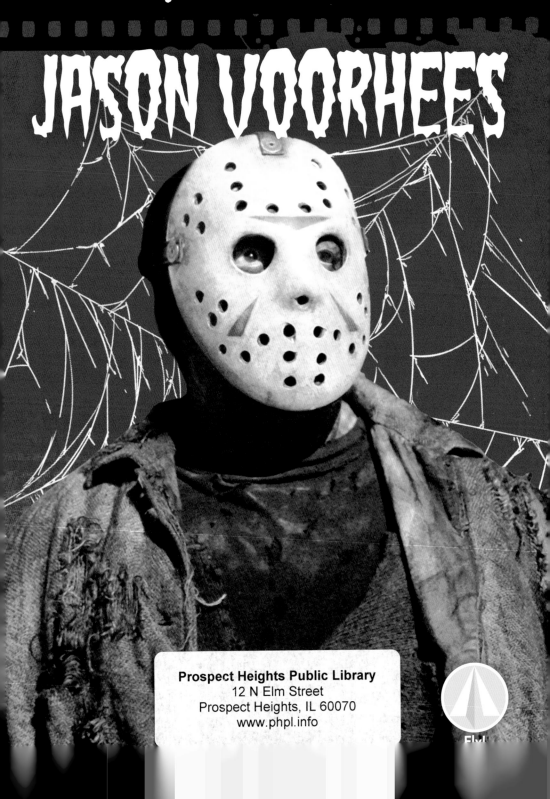

JASON VOORHEES

abdobooks.com

Published by Abdo Zoom, a division of ABDO, P.O. Box 398166, Minneapolis, Minnesota 55439. Copyright © 2020 by Abdo Consulting Group, Inc. International copyrights reserved in all countries. No part of this book may be reproduced in any form without written permission from the publisher. Fly!™ is a trademark and logo of Abdo Zoom.

Printed in the United States of America, North Mankato, Minnesota.
052019
092019

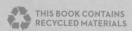

Photo Credits: Alamy, Everette Collection, Shutterstock
Production Contributors: Kenny Abdo, Jennie Forsberg, Grace Hansen
Design Contributors: Dorothy Toth, Neil Klinepier

Library of Congress Control Number: 2018963569

Publisher's Cataloging-in-Publication Data

Names: Abdo, Kenny, author.
Title: Jason Voorhees / by Kenny Abdo.
Description: Minneapolis, Minnesota : Abdo Zoom, 2020 | Series: Hollywood monsters set 2 | Includes online resources and index.
Identifiers: ISBN 9781532127465 (lib. bdg.) | ISBN 9781532128448 (ebook) | ISBN 9781532128936 (Read-to-me ebook)
Subjects: LCSH: Voorhees, Jason (Fictitious character)--Juvenile literature. | Friday the 13th (Motion picture)--Juvenile literature. | Horror films-- Juvenile literature. | Motion picture characters--Juvenile literature.
Classification: DDC 791.43616--dc23

TABLE OF CONTENTS

JASON VOORHEES

Friday the 13th is a 1980s
movie about Jason Voorhees.
As a child, he drowned while at
summer camp. His counselors
were not watching him. After
many years, Jason comes back
for his revenge.

Known for his frightening hockey mask and machete, Jason Voorhees is one of the most recognized slashers in horror cinema.

ORIGIN

Screenwriter Victor Miller saw the success of the horror movie *Halloween*. He had his own idea. His was one that took place at a summer camp where nobody was safe.

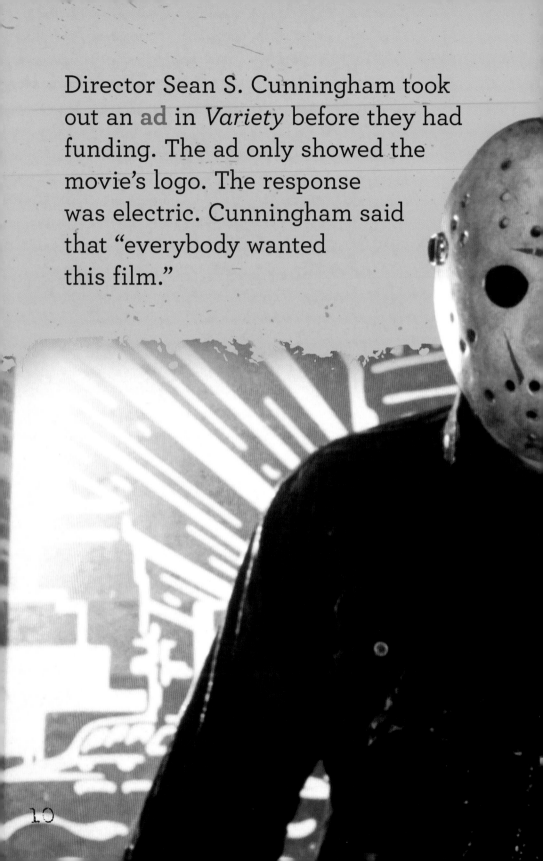

Director Sean S. Cunningham took out an **ad** in *Variety* before they had funding. The ad only showed the movie's logo. The response was electric. Cunningham said that "everybody wanted this film."

Jason was originally named Josh. Producers thought that wasn't scary enough. So, Miller changed it to Jason after someone who once bullied him.

HOLLYWOOD

Friday the 13th was not supposed to be a **franchise**. Because of that, Jason was not the original villain. It was his mother, Pamela Voorhees.

13

The movie was very unpopular with reviewers. Gene Siskel, a film critic, gave away the **twist** ending on his popular TV show.

Despite the negative reviews, it was a monster hit! Audiences went wild for the **twist** ending. **Special-effects** artist Tom Savani would go to screenings just to watch viewers jump.

The studio decided to bring adult
Jason back as the **antagonist** for the
remainder of the **sequels**.

Jason is seen wearing his iconic hockey mask for the first time an hour into *Friday the 13th Part III*. It was suggested by a crew member who was an avid Detroit Red Wings fan.

LEGACY

There are 12 movies in the *Friday the 13th* **franchise**. Not all of them take place at Camp Crystal Lake. One took Jason to Manhattan, New York. Another took him into space!

Jason claims more than 160 victims throughout the series. That is more than any slasher in horror movie history!

LeBron James is working on producing a *Friday the 13th* reboot. He believes Jason has unfinished business at Camp Crystal Lake!

GLOSSARY

ad – a short message in print or on television or radio that helps sell a product.

antagonist – the main villain in a story.

franchise – a collection of related movies in a series.

reboot – a new start to a movie franchise, recreating plots, characters, and backstory.

screenwriter – the person who writes the story and dialogue for a movie.

sequel – a movie, or other work that continues the story begun in a preceding one.

special effect – artificial visual effects used to create illusions on film.

twist – a major change in direction of the story of a movie.

ONLINE RESOURCES

Booklinks
NONFICTION NETWORK
FREE! ONLINE NONFICTION RESOURCES

To learn more about
Jason Voorhees, please visit
abdobooklinks.com or scan
this QR code. These links
are routinely monitored and
updated to provide the most
current information available.

INDEX